## Piper's Dictionary

### A

**a mach.** Literally translated from gaelic, means "to go out." Used in context of describing complex piobaireachd variations, such as "<u>taorluath a mach</u>" or "<u>crunluath a mach</u>." Only executed from B, C and D. The "a mach" variations are typically the last ones in a piobaireachd. Prounced *"ah mahk."*

**AB.** *(abbreviation)* African Blackwood. See "<u>African Blackwood</u>."

**abc.** A text based notation for music. For instance, Low-A is "A", High-A is "a", grace notes are indicated by placing them in curly braces, e.g. {g} is a High-G grace note. For a complete description visit <u>The abc home page</u>

**ABW.** *(abbreviation)* African Blackwood. See "<u>African Blackwood</u>."

**acciaccatura.** A fancy Latin term for a grace note, not commonly used by pipers. See *"<u>grace note</u>."*

**ACPBA.** *(abbreviation)* Atlantic Canada Pipe Band Association. <u>acpba.ednet.ns.ca</u>

**active grace note.** A grace note in a movement that is sounded by raising the finger associated with that note, for example, the "G" and "F" graces in an E doubling. As opposed to a "static grace note." This somewhat uncommon term is seen in "The College of Piping Tutor For The Highland Bagpipe: Part 3." Also see "*static grace note.*"

**adjudicator.** A judge of competitions.

**African Blackwood.** The most common wood used for making bagpipes. Contains natural oils excellent for accoustic performance. Known as the *Mpingo* tree in the KiSwahili language.

**AGL.** *(abbreviation)* Above Grade Level. A comment (sometimes a checkbox) found on competition judging forms. If the judge feels that the particular performance was above the grade in which it was played, they can indicate so. Helps an association evaluate whether someone is capable of advancing to a higher grade.

**Aiguillette.** Ornamental braiding worn at the shoulder. Similar to fancy shoelaces in appearance.

**Airstream.** A brand of plastic blowpipe and somewhat rectangular-shaped mouthpiece.

**alternate attack note.** Any note other than "E" as the introductory (non-melody) note of a band set. While not common, it's acceptable in most competitions, though if done less than perfectly will normally result in a bigger deduction than a failed "E" attack note. If done well, it can be rewarded by the judges. Can be considered a "gimmick" by traditional judges. *Also see "attack note."*

**Argyll.** A type of very plain cut doublet jacket. Not as common. Named after Clan Campbell of Argyle/Argyll, a former county in western Scotland. Prounced *"R guy L."*

**Argyllshire Gathering.** A annual high-profile competition and games held in Oban, Scotland. Founded in 1871.

**Arr.** *(abbreviation)* Arranged. *See "arranged."*

**arranged.** Refers to an individual (not the composer) who wrote down a particular version (arrangement) of a tune. For example, a tune may be noted as: "Arranged PM D. MacLeod," this means the particular combination of gracenotes, etc. was decided by this individual. Often abbreviated "Arr."

**attack.** Usually used with regard to bands, refers to the beginning of a performance. For instance: "We blew the attack, one of the pipers started playing the wrong tune."

**attack note.** The introductory note of a band set. Bands typically strike in the drones, sound an "E" note (the common attack note), then follow with the first note of the tune. *Also see "alternate attack note."*

# B

**bag.** An airtight sack of sorts to which the stocks are secured. Traditionally made of sheepskin or cowhide, now also made of Gortex and other synthetics or combination of a synthetic interior and a hide exterior.

**bag cover.** A decorative fabric sleeve into which the bag is inserted. The fabric is commonly velvet, corduroy or a tartan, but others are also used. Fringe at each of the openings (chanter stock, drone stocks, blowpipe stock and rear) is common.

**Bakelite.** An early non-flammable plastic used for some early 20th century bagpipe mounts. Patented by Dr. Leo Baekeland (Belgian born) around 1910, who started the Bakelite Corporation. Formed from a combination of carbolic acid and formaldehyde to produce phenolic resin dubbed "Bakelite." Bakelite replaced flammable celluloid, which had been the most popular synthetic material. Bakelite came in the five colors of yellow, brown, butterscotch, green and red—the later two of which were not commonly used in bagpipe making. Bakelite usually changes color within few years after its manufacture and can be found to be relatively dark on old sets. Starting in the 1920s cylinders of the material were cast and from which mounts would be turned. The Bakelite patent expired in 1927 and was immediately acquired by the Catalin Corporation which renamed the product "Catalin" and developed a process to allow for a total of twenty colors. Bakelite and Catalin became obsolete by the end of WWII.

**baldric.** A heavily ornamented piece of fabric worn diagonally across the chest. Used to identify the individual in charge, typically worn by the drum major or in his/her absence, the pipe major. If the band wears duty sashes, the band leader would wear a baldric and a duty sash. Also see "<u>duty sash</u>."

**balmoral.** A type of headwear, somewhat like a mushroom in shape, typically with a decorative ball in the center on top. Often seen with a metal badge on one side and two ribbons that dangle at the back.

**Bannatyne.** A brand of synthetic bagpipe bag available either as a fully synthetic bag or a synthetic bag with incorporated hide outer layer.

**bar.** In sheet music, it is a portion of the tune between two vertical line dividers on the staff. The number of beats in a bar is indicated by the time signature.

**bass drone.** The longest drone on a set of bagpipes, when tuned sounds exactly two octaves lower than Low-A on the chanter.

**bass drum.** Large low-pitched drum that sets the beat. A bass drummer plays both sides (heads) while the drum is held in a vertical position.

**BD.** *(abbreviation)* Break down. See "<u>break down</u>."

**beading.** The wider areas between the combing on a drone. *Also see "combing."*

**bell.** The dramatically wider portion at the top of a drone, may also refer to the internal bore which is resembles an upside-down bell.

**BEM.** *(abbreviation)* British Empire Medal. Was a lower-class form of the MBE. Eliminated by the British Prime Minister in the 1990's as it was considered to be socially wrong to have what could be considered a two-tier system. *Also see "MBE" and "OBE."*

**Big Mac.** *See "Bor Mor."*

**binding.** The black hemp used to wrap the two pieces of cane to the staple of chanter reed.

**birl.** A movement that starts from Low-A, with the pinky tapping to sound Low-G, sounding Low-A, then the pinky immediately and quickly drawn completely across the Low-A hole to briefly sound Low-G then Low-A. This technique is called "tap and pull." Variations in execution include the "7" style where the pinky is passed down over the Low-A hole then pulled across, or a slide method of simply passing the pinky down then up across the Low-A hole.

**blackwood.** See "*African blackwood.*"

**blade.** A piece of curved cane, two of which form the vibrating surfaces of a chanter reed. Sometimes called "a tongue."

**blowpipe.** Used to get air from the piper's mouth to the bag. One end of the blowpipe is fitted with a replaceable mouthpiece and the other is fitted with a flapper valve.

**blowpipe valve.** Sometimes called a flapper valve, this keeps the air from coming back out of the bag through the blowpipe. Traditionally made of leather, commerical valves—such as the Li'l Mac—are made of rubber, plastic and metal. Sometimes fabricated out of electrical tape in a pinch. Also sometimes called a "clack valve."

**blue book.** Part 3 of The Highland Bagpipe Tutor by Seumas MacNeill and Thomas Pearston published by the College of Piping, Glasgow, Scotland. Discussion continues where Part 1 leaves off. Traditionally has been printed with a blue cover. Part 1 has a green cover, Part 2 has a red cover.

**BMW.** *(abbreviation)* Bagpipe Music Writer. A software program for writing pipe music.

Bagpipe Music Writer Gold files end with the suffix ".bww". The older BagpipeMusic Writer files end in ".bmw".

**boards.** A judging area at a competition. In some cases, it can be raised wooden stage. In others, simply a designated patch of ground.

**bonnet.** A type of tall headwear usually adored with lots of feathers, typically worn only with elaborate piping regalia.

**Bor Mor.** A brand of blowpipe flapper valve. Made by Cushing Bagpipes. Nicknamed the "Big Mac."

**border pipes.** Conical bore bellows-blown pipes of the Scottish "Border" region.

**bore.** The opening that passes through the length of a drone or chanter.

**BPM.** *(abbreviation)* Beats Per Minute.

**Braemar.** Prounced *"bray-mar."* A type of very plain cut doublet jacket, similar to an Argyll. Not as common. Named after Clan Campbell of Argyle/Argyll, a former county in western Scotland.

**Bratach Gorm.** An prestigious annual competition sponsored by The Scottish Piping Society of London.

**break down.** Failure to complete a tune. Usually in competition. Sometimes seen abbreviated on judging sheets as "BD."

**bridle.** A ring of material used on reeds to control pitch by changing the amount of vibrating surface. Usually either hemp or a rubber-band like object.

**bright.** A term used to describe a chanter that is easily heard against the drones.

**bubble note.** See "*darado*."

**bush.** The material attached at the very top end of a drone, usually silver, ivory or a synthetic ivory. Mellows the sound coming from the drone. Also called a "drone cap" or "bushing."

**bushing.** See "*bush*."

**BWW.** File name extention for Bagpipe Music Writer Gold. *Also see "BMW."*

**by the center.** This is a directive from the leader of a band on where the band is to "take their dressing," that is, who to use as their reference in marching with regard to matching their footwork. In this case, "the center" would be a drum major marching out in front and center of the band. *Also see "by the right."*

**by the right.** This is a directive from the leader of a band on where the band is to "take their dressing," that is, who to use as their reference in marching with regard to matching their footwork. In this case, "the right" would be a pipe major, the rightmost and frontmost player. *Also see "by the center."*

## C

**C.** *(abbreviation)* Common time. Sometimes "C" is used instead of "4/4" to indicate the time signature.

**C.** *(abbreviation)* Crunluath. Used in the context of music notation for piobaireachd. Rather than writing out the notes for all the crunluath embellishments in a crunluath variation, a letter "C" is used.

**caber.** A long, very heavy pole used in the Scottish athletic event, caber tossing. The basic objective is to throw the caber end over end, which requires quite a bit of strength.

**cadence.** A short series of notes common in piobaireachd: High-G gracenote to E, D gracenote to B, followed by Low-G gracenote to A. Usually found at the end of a phrase.

**cane.** *arundo donax*, native to circummediterranean areas but now introduced to temperate regions, is used for making chanter and drone reeds. Not to be confused with bamboo which is not used in piping.

**Canmore.** A brand of synthetic bagpipe bag.

**cannister bag.** A bag that utilizes a dessicant cannister to trap moisture through a series of internal hoses to and from the various stocks. Bag must allow for access via zipper or clamp in order to recharge the dessicant (which is sometimes simply "kitty litter").

**canntaireachd.** A system for verbal transmission of bagpipe music in which notes and embellishments have been assigned unique sounds and names, such as "Cherede,"

"Hihorodo," and "Endre." Prounced *"can ter ock."* Also see *"vocable."*

**cap.** *See "reed cap" or "drone cap."*

**catch.** Another name for a crossing noise, but usually applies to one created by incorrectly changing notes on the same hand. *Also see "crossing noise."*

**caubeen.** An Irish cap, which could be described as a larger more puffy beret, sometimes seen with a emblem on the front face and small plume at the crown. Usually worn with the high point either centered over the forehead or over the left eye. Pronounced *"kaw-bean,"* rhymes with *"saw-seen."*

**cauld wind.** Bellows-blown.

**CBE.** *(abbreviation)* Commander of the Order of the British Empire. A British distinguished honor. *Also see O.B.E., M.B.E., B.E.M.*

**ceilidh.** Loosely translates to "party" in Gaelic. Pronounced *"kay lee."*

**cent.** A unit of change in pitch, usually used in context of a electronic tuner. 1200 cents equal one octave in the twelve note chromatic scale, 100 cents equals a half step between notes. The value of cent in hertz (Hz) will change depending on where the note is in the scale, but for a chanter can usually be considered between approximately 0.25Hz (Low-A) and 0.5Hz (High-A). The human ear cannot differentiate less than 5 cents.

**ceòl beag.** Means "little music" in Gaelic, refers to non-piobaireachd compositions such as reels, jigs, marches, etc. Pronounced *"kyawl bake"* or *"kyawl buck."*

**ceòl mór.** In Gaelic, means "big music," referring to piobaireachd. Pronounced *"kyawl more."* Also see "piobaireachd."

**chalice top.** A less common contoured design for the transition down from the bell to the rest of the upper drone section. Resembles the round nature of a wine glass or chalice vs. a noticable step.

**chanter.** The portion of a set of bagpipes upon which the piper produces the melody of a tune by opening and closing holes with his/her fingers. Sometimes called a "pipe chanter."

**chanter cap.** *See "reed cap."*

**choke.** The circumstance when the chanter reed stops sounding unintentionally.

**chromatic scale.** A scale composed of twelve notes.

**CITES.** *(abbreviation)* Convention on International Trade in Endandered Species. Typically referring to a mandatory permit to allow international transport of elephant ivory mounted bagpipes, such as "I'm going to Canada, I have my CITES [or CITES certificate] for my old pipes ready to go." One can apply for a permit (often temporary) to allow restricted material to be transported under specific conditions.

**clan.** A group of families from the same common Scottish Highlands ancestor. Each clan has one or more associated tartans. *Also see "tartan."*

**Clasp, The.** While there are other "clasp" events, this usually refers to the annual world-level piobaireachd competition, the Northern Gathering/Northern Meeting held in Inverness, Scotland. Only holders of the Highland Society of London's Gold Medal can compete for The

Clasp at Inverness, and the Senior Piobaireachd at Oban, both being "former winners" events.

**classical music.** Another name for piobaireachd. *See "piobaireachd."*

**claymore.** A large double-edged Scottish sword usually worn on one's back.

**CM.** *(abbreviation)* The Order of Canada, one of the highest honors awarded to a Canadian civilian.

**CNC.** *(abbreviation)* Computer numerical control. Seen in descriptions of manufacturing, refers to equipment controlled by computer, such as automated turning of bagpipes or synthetic reeds.

**cockage.** An ornamental rosette or knot of ribbon found on the front of a balmoral or on the side of a glengarry. For non-civilians, can used to indicate military or naval service.

**combing.** The fine parallel ornamental ring grooves carved into parts of a bagpipe. *Also see "beading."*

**common time.** Another name for the 4/4 time signature. Sometimes seen indicated as "C" or a cent symbol instead of "4/4" on musical notation.

**conical bore.** A bore that tapers from a small diameter at one end to a larger one. Also called a "tapered bore." *Also see "bore."*

**COP.** *(abbreviation)* College of Piping in Glasgow, Scotland. Also seen abbreviated "C of P."

**cord holder.** Located toward the top of each drone, the channel formed by two protruding rings of wood about which the drone cords are fastened.

**cords.** *See "drone cords."*

**cork.** 1) A rubber or cork stopper used to plug either the top of a drone or one of the stocks. 2) Material traditionally used, but no longer common, to cover tenons. *Also see "tenon."*

**CPA.** *(abbreviation)* Competing Pipers Association, based in Scotland. Founded in the mid-1970s.

**crit sheet.** Short for "critique sheet." Another name for a competition scoring sheet.

**cross fingering.** Holding one's fingers in a uncommon position in order to yield a note not of the standard nine chanter notes, i.e. C-natural.

**cross handed.** When a piper plays with the bag side hand lower on the chanter than the other—very uncommon. Typically the arm holding the bag has that hand playing the higher chanter notes. Not to be confused with a left-handed piper, who might hold the bag under the right arm with the right hand playing the top notes, a situation that is not considered cross handed.

**crossbelt.** Leather belt worn across the chest—top right to bottom left—with the buckle positioned at the right chest.

**crossing noise.** An undesirable interim note that sounds when changing from one note to another. Most common when changing from a bottom hand note to a top hand note, but can also sound from the same hand. *Also see "catch."*

**crow.** A rough squawking of sorts that sounds on a High-A, the desire for which varies from piper to piper by taste. Can allow the High-A to be heard more easily against the louder drones. Often times can be reduced by blowing harder or lightly sanding the chanter reed blade tips.

**crunluath.** A combination of grace notes forming an embelishment. Melody note, followed by the gracenotes Low-G, D, Low-G, E, Low-A, F, Low-A then always ending on E. From D, a B note is typically substituted for the D gracing. Common in Piobaireachd, but not light music. In Gaelic, "luath" means "quick." "Crun" is thought to be a variation of "crown." The "king of quick embellishments" perhaps. Pronouced *"crun-LOO-ah."*

**crunluath a mach.** Only executed from B, C and D. From B, the following series of gracenotes: Low-G, D, Low-G, B, E, B, F, B, ending on E. From C, the following series of gracenotes: Low-G, D, Low-G, C, E, C, F, C, ending on E. From D, the following series of gracenotes: High-G, B, D-throw, E, D, F, D, ending on E. *(Yes, long and convoluted, best consult your instructor or book.)* Pronouced *"crun-LOO-ah ah mahk."*

**crunluath breabach.** Same as the crunluath, with an addition of two notes, depending on context. *(Full details would be long and convoluted, consult your instructor or book.)* Pronouced *"crun-LOO-ah BRAY-buhk"*.

**crunluath doubling.** A doubling variation that is played with crunluaths. Term applies to piobaireachd tunes.

**crunluath fosgailte.** There's four of these, each starting different but each ending with the crunluath ending, that is, gracenotes: E, Low-A, F, Low-A to E melody note. 1) Himdandre is: High-G, Low-G, D, Low-A plus ending. 2) Hintodre is: Low-A, D, B plus ending. 3) Hindodre is: High-G, D, C, plus ending. 4) Hindadre is: High-G, Low-A, D, plus ending. *(Yes, long and convoluted, best consult your instructor or book.)* Pronouced *"crun-LOO-ah FOSS-kiltch"*.

**cuff.** A separate piece of attire that is slipped over the top of the hose to accentuate the folded portion of the hose. Perhaps most commonly takes the form of a "popcorn top." *Also see "popcorn top."*

**cut off.** The instant at the end of a tune when the drones stop sounding. A clean cut off is when the drones instantly go from in pitch to silent. *Also see "trailing drones."*

**cut out.** The circumstance when a reed stops sounding, either intentionally or unintentionally.

## D

**D-throw.** An embellishment, also called a "throw on D". The so-called "light D-throw" is more common: melody note, followed by gracenotes: Low-G, D, C, ending on melody note D. The "heavy D-throw" is: melody note, followed by gracenotes: Low-G, D, Low-G, C, ending on melody note D.

**darado.** A somewhat rare embellishment. Melody note followed by gracenotes: Low-G, D, Low-G, C, Low-G to the ending melody note. Sometimes called a "bubble/bubbly note." Pronounced *"DAH-ra-do."*

**day wear.** Informal attire. In the case of a sporran, a plain style such as tooled leather.

**day wear plaid.** An unpleated/unsewn piper's plaid folded to reduce the length by half, then folded the short direction in half twice to one quarter of it's original width. This is placed over the left shoulder with the fringed end hanging down at the front. Basically, a blanket folded and thrown over your shoulder. Not to be confused with a "fly plaid." *Also see "fly plaid".*

**DCM.** *(abbreviation)* Distinguished Conduct Medal.

**deburring tool.** A metal tool used to carve out chanter holes. Sometimes used to fine tune a hole after filing with a riffler file. *Also see "riffler file."*

**Delrin.** This synthetic (acetal resin) is used as a replacement for traditional wood in the manufacture of bagpipes and practice chanters. Delrin is a registered trademark of DuPont. *Also see "Polypenco."*

**dial manometer.** *See "manometer."*

**dicing.** A checkerboard-like pattern found on glengarries, bonnets and hose, typically of alternating two or three colors. Red and white is a very common pattern as is red, white and navy blue.

**dirge.** A funeral song or tune. Comes from the first word in a Latin funeral rite. Used by some pipers as a derogatory term, such as "that wasn't a lament, that was a dirge." Pronouced *"derj."*

**dirk.** A long knife, usually worn at the waist. Considerably larger than a sgian dubh.

**dithis.** The name applied to a piobaireachd variation if it meets the following criteria: Each long theme note is followed by a short low-A. The long theme note is preceded by a G gracenote unless it's high-G (thumb gracenote) or High-A (no gracing). The short low-A is preceded by an E gracenote, except E and F (G gracenote), high-G (thumb gracenote), and high-A (no gracing). A dithis variation is played in a pointed manner. In Gaelic, "dithis" means a pairing of two men. Pronounced *"JEE-ish."* Also see *"dithis doubling."*

**dithis doubling.** The name applied to a piobaireachd variation if it meets the same criteria as a dithis, *but* instead of a short low-A being played, a short repeat of the theme note is played. "Dithis" is pronounced *"JEE-ish."* See *"dithis."*

**double echo beat.** A strike followed after a brief pause by slightly longer strike to the same note, giving the impression of "call and response."

**doublet.** A close-fitting formal jacket. *Also see "Montrose doublet."*

**doubling.** 1) The embellishment of a note, composed of a High-G gracenote, followed by a D gracenote and ending on the melody note. ("B doubling.") 2) A type of variation on the ground of a piobaireachd. ("Doubling of the ground.")

**dressing.** 1) When marching, a band addresses to (or "takes its dressing from") an individual, usually the drum major or pipe major, from whom it takes direction on footwork. *Also see "by the center" and "by the right."* 2) Another name for "*seasoning*."

**drone cap.** *See "bush"*

**drone cords.** Rope-like material, with tassles on the two ends, used to secure drones into position.

**drone lock.** An informal reference to the condition of drones being perfectly tuned.

**drone valve.** Typically placed at the base of the drone stock inside the bag to help regulate air through the drones, the intent of these is to stabilize changes in bag pressure with regard to the drone reeds, so the piper has steadier sound and easier starts and crisp stops. Volume is reduced slightly. Only practical with a zipper or clamp-back bags.

**drones.** The three large wooden "tubes" tied together by cords on a set of great highland bagpipes, each continually plays a single note.

**drum major.** The individual with the mace at the front of a marching band. Yells commands, leads the band. Band follows his command though he will often take his lead from the pipe major. Abbreviated "DM."

**drum sergeant.** Lead drummer in a band, other drummers their drumming specific cues from this person. Sometimes also called a "lead stroke," or "lead drummer." Often seen abbreviated as "DS."

**drummer's plaid.** A large squarish fringed piece of tartan material that is draped over the left shoulder with a brooch at the front, attached at the waist in the rear and secured by buttoning a hidden loop to the epaulet button. Smaller than a full plaid and larger (longer) than a fly plaid. A full (piper's) plaid could interfere with drum harnesses and as such are sometimes not worn by drummers, though some bands require their drummers to wear a full plaid regardless. Also known as a "half plaid."

**dry stock.** See "*reed cap.*"

**DS, D/S, D.S.** *(abbreviation)* Drum sergeant.

**duty sash.** A wide piece of fabric (often red) worn around the waist or diagonally across the chest from the left shoulder to the right hip in pipe bands. (Originally used to hold sword scabbards, military units wear the sash from the right shoulder to the left hip.) Usually worn by the drum/pipe sergeants and drum/pipe majors. *Also see "baldric."*

**Dycem®.** A "non-slip" synthetic sheet ("Non-Slip Reel") used in patches on the exterior of bag covers to prevent slipping. To apply, either hand sew or temporarily place wax paper over it when using a sewing machine. Non-toxic. Cleans with soap and water when it loses its stickiness. Dycem.com DycemShop

# E

**EC.** *(abbreviation)* Executive Committee, as in the governing board of an association. Includes executive members such as a president, vice-president, secretary, treasurer, registrar, past president.

**echo.** A less common term with the same meaning as "tap" or "strike." *Also see "strike" or "double echo beat."*

**edre.** A movement. A melody note followed by these gracenotes: E, Low-A, F, Low-A to E. Always ends on melody note E.

**elk hide.** Cow hide has been treated using "elk tanning process." (Not from the elk animal.) Commonly used for bagpipe bags.

**embellishment.** A grace note or combination of grace notes that accent the following melody note.

**end plug.** A long plug located at the unseated end of a synthetic drone reed, which is slid in or out to adjust the pitch of the reed and is usually held in place by friction. Found on Ross brand drone reeds, for example. Most synthetic reeds use a threaded plug called a tuning screw. *Also see "tuning screw."*

**engraving.** Taking a less presentable tune manuscript and creating a polished-looking tune sheet. As in "music engraving."

**epaulet strap.** On a dress jacket, a strip of fabric with one end sewn into the seam where the sleeve meets the shoulder and the other end fastened by a button near the collar. Also simply called an "epaulet."

**evening wear.** Formal attire. In the case of a sporran, a more elaborate style, such as animal fur with polished metal top.

**expression.** As in "expressing" the tune. Since bagpipes cannot alter the volume of the notes or introduce silence, and to be true to the tune you cannot change the notes, the only thing left is holding notes longer or cutting them shorter to enhance the feel of the tune, such as exaggerating the "swing" of a tune. Done properly, this altering of the note values gives the tune more expression.

F

**false fingering.** Playing a note with the correct top hole open, but at least one or more lower holes either open or closed incorrectly, yielding a note that can sound slightly or substantially off.

**ferrule.** Metal rings located at the end of a stock or drone cylinder to keep the wood from swelling and splitting; usually composed of nickel, silver, ivory or a synthetic ivory.

**file.** Refers to a band in formation, a line of players arranged one behind another, front to back. Also sometimes called a "column." (As opposed to a _row_.)

**Fireside Pipes.** A brand name of parlor pipes made by Gibson.

**flapper valve.** See _"blowpipe valve."_

**flashes.** Much like little flags, these bits of fabric (commonly matching or color coordinating with the kilt) hang out from under the top of hose, on the outside of the calf and are held in place with a garter.

**flat.** A note is considered _flat_ if it is below (deeper sounding than) the expected pitch.

**fly plaid.** This plaid is made from a roughly square fringed piece of tartan (40"x40" and 40"x52" are sizes you may see), stitched in one corner which is pinned at the front of the shoulder while the rest is "thrown" over the shoulder and hangs at the back. Not usually attire for a band. Smaller than a drummer's plaid. Also see "drummer's plaid" and "mini fly plaid."

**FMM.** *(abbreviation)* Field Marshall Mongmery Pipe Band. A Grade I band based in Northern Ireland.

**forked A.** Another name for a High-A note played with the F finger down, the G and E fingers being the "prongs of the fork." Also known as a "piobaireachd High-A."

**forked G.** Another name for a High-G note played with the F finger down, the G and E fingers being the "prongs of the fork." Also known as a "piobaireachd High-G."

**forked movement.** Refers to either a High-A or a High-G note played with the F finger down, the G and E fingers being the "prongs of the fork."

**fosgailte.** "opened, unbarred, unbolted" in Gaelic. Seen in context such as "crunluath fosgailte." Pronouced *"FOSS-kiltch." Also see "crunluath fosgailte."*

**full-mounted.** Refers to when all the ivory/synthetic/silver/wood ornamentation on the *projecting mounts*, *ferrules* and *bushes* are made of the same material.

**full plaid.** See *"piper's plaid."*

**fundamental.** Short for "fundamental frequency." *See "harmonic."*

# G

**GHB.** *(abbreviation)* Great Highland Bagpipes.

**gillie brogues.** A type of footwear worn by pipers. Appears at first glance to be a dress shoe with the tongue removed. Sometimes incorrectly referred to as "gillies" which in Scottish means only "young boy." Pronounced *"gill-ee bro-gs."*

**glengarry.** A type of headwear, a brimless hat, with flat sides, is pleated from front to back and folds flat along that axis. Often seen with a metal badge on one side and two ribbons that dangle at the back.

**goose.** A type of bagpipe with only a chanter and no drones, used for practice. One can make a goose of a full set of bagpipes by plugging the drone stocks.

**goose adapter.** This fitting allows the bottom section of a practice chanter to connect to the chanter stock of a full set of pipes. This along with plugging the drones, creates an easily played goose out of a full set of pipes.

**grace note.** A very quick note used to embellish the note which follows either a melody note or another gracenote. While indicated on piping sheet music as a 1/32th note, these notes take no time with regard to the beat. The beam on these notes always points up, unlike melody notes where the beam always point down.

**grade.** A competence level applied to competing pipers. Grade 5 is practice chanter only. Grade 4 is beginning piper (about 75% of competing pipers never graduate from this grade), followed by Grade 3, Grade 2, and Grade 1. Beyond Grade 1 is "open" or "professional," the non-amateur classification. Grading is determined by a piping association.

**great music.** Another name for piobaireachd. See *"piobaireachd."*

**green book.** Part 1 of The Highland Bagpipe Tutor by Seumas MacNeill and Thomas Pearston published by the College of Piping, Glasgow, Scotland. Basic introduction to playing the bagpipe. Traditionally has been printed with a green cover. Part 2 has a red cover, Part 3 has a blue cover.

**grip.** Modern name for "leumluath" movement. See *"leumluath."*

**ground.** The inital part or "main theme" of a piobaireachd tune. In Scottish, called the "urlar."

**gut buster.** Slang term for a very hard chanter reed.

# H

**HA.** *(abbreviation)* High A. Somewhat uncommon in usage.

**hackle.** Bird plumage used as an accessory to headwear.

**haggis.** A form of Scottish sausage historically stuffed with oatmeal and meat of questionable origin, e.g. animal guts. These days, they are often made of better materials.

**half-doubling.** A doubling executed from High-A or High-G, in which the usual G gracenote is necessarily omitted.

**half-mounted.** Refers to when all the ivory/ synthetic/silver/wood ornamentation on the projecting mounts, ferrules and caps are not made of the same material. Usually less costly than a full-mounted set of pipes.

**half plaid.** See *"drummer's plaid."*

**hallmark.** A series of stamps found on valuable metals from the UK. These symbols attest to the quality of the metal, the location where the metal was tested, the identity of the metal smith/ sponsor, and the year of testing.

**harmonic.** A fundamental (or "fundamental frequency" or "first harmonic") is the lowest frequency (longest wavelength) in a sound (note) generated by a musical instrument, such as a bagpipe chanter or drone. Also produced are "overtones" (higher order harmonics), which are quieter, higher frequencies of "integral multiples" (multiplied by integers/whole numbers) of the fundamental such as "x2", "x3", "x4", etc., the first of which is the "second harmonic" which is two times (2x) the frequency of the fundamental. Notes an octave apart will be either 1/2x or 2x of each other, e.g. a chanter high-A frequency will be two times that of chanter low-A frequency and chanter low-A frequency will be one half of that of a properly tuned tenor's A.

**head**. The playing surface of a drum.

**heavy D-Throw.** See *"D-throw."*

**heel balm.** A home-made wood putty used by some pipemakers, usually a mixture of African Blackwood and an adhesive. It is used to fill defects in a bagpipe. One such less honorable use is to fill up gaps between a bagpipe part and its matching outside piece (ferrule, ring cap), the gap created by over-turning the wood until it is too small. A high quality new bagpipe would not require this fix as the pieces would correctly match.

**hemp.** Heavy string used to hold adjustable parts of the bagpipe in place, such as at the base of a chanter reed or on the drone sliders. Once placed, is often referred to as "hemping," e.g. "The hemping of your drone pin is loose and must be redone."

**hemp stop.** The raised area at the very end of a tuning pin just past the tenon which serves as the upper barrier for the hemping. (The lower barrier being the main body of the tuning pin itself.)

**HG.** *(abbreviation)* High G. Somewhat uncommon in usage.

**HLI.** *(abbreviation)* Highland Light Infantry.

**hornpipe.** A type of music. In piping, this term does not refer to the rare old instrument of the same name. Usually in 2/4 time.

**hose.** The long socks worn by pipers, traditional styles require folding over twice at the top. Also called "kilt hose."

**hose tops.** Pipers "partial socks" that cover the leg from below the knee to the ankle. Intended to be used with everyday socks that are hidden with spats. *Also see "spats."*

**Hz.** *(abbreviation)* Hertz. Cycles per second, a description of frequency. In terms of acoustics, number of sound wave cycles per second. Used to decribe the pitch of a note, which can be measured with a sound meter, or "tuner." *Also see "tuner."*

I

**Institute of Piping.** A collaberation of The Piobaireachd Society, The Army School of Bagpipe Music, The College of Piping, and The Piping Centre. Puts forth a standardized piping certificate program.

**Inverness.** A city in Scotland, home of the annual Northern Gathering. *Also see "Northern Gathering."*

**Irish war pipes.** Virtually identical to the Great Highland Bagpipes, but has a two drones (bass and single tenor) instead of a three drones.

**IvoryPlus.** A natural ivory substitute, the Carolina Palm Nut grows on the Caroline Islands in Micronesia. Sometimes tagua nuts can also be used, but are typically too small for projecting mounts on bagpipes.

## J

**jabot shirt.** Old-style shirt with lace material hanging from the neck to mid-chest in a waterfall-like fashion, with long lace trim at the wrists.

**jacobite shirt.** Old-style collared loose-fitting shirt that closes with a drawstring at the neck, with sleeves the bunch up with extra fabric at the the wrist. Typically made of muslin.

**jig.** A type of tune with a quick beat, usually in 6/8 time.

## K

**Kenmore.** A type of doublet. Not as common.

**kilt.** The traditional attire of the Scottish Highlands. The modern "half-kilt" is composed of a long length of plaid material that is pleated and bound just above the waist. Sometimes intentionally used incorrectly as a verb, such as "Many men were 'kilt' for calling it a dress."

**kilt hose.** See *"hose."*

**kirking the tartan.** A church service involving a tartan procession into the church, a prayer service and a recessional utilizing bagpiping. This purely American ceremony was contrived Reverend Peter Mashall in the early 1940s in Washington D.C. It's original function was to promote bonds to finance the Allied war effort.

**kitchen pipes.** A small quiet bagpipe of sorts, basically a practice chanter fitted to a bag with some rudimentary drones.

**kitchen piping.** Bagpiping with a loose knit group of people, perhaps a one time "jam" session, perhaps with a selection of instruments that is not traditionally played with the pipes.

**L**

**LA.** *(abbreviation)* Low A. Somewhat uncommon in usage.

**lance corporal.** First level of supervision over "regular" pipers and drummers in a band, each of whom would be considered a "private." Subordinate to a "corporal" and any member bearing a title with the word "sergeant" or "major" in it. Looks after any small jobs that the Pipe Sergeant or Drum Sergeant have issued (or indirectly issued by the Pipe or Drum Majors). Also called a "Pipe Corporal." *[Note: There's some contention regarding pipe corporal vs. corporal vs. lance corporal, I'm looking into this and will be updating this entry at some point.]*

**lathe.** A machine that spins a length of wood around its shortest axis so that it may be shaped with various gouges and other tools. Used by a turner to create each part of the bagpipe. Also called a "wood lathe."

**LD.** *(abbreviation)* Lead Drummer. See *"drum sergeant."*

**lead drummer.** See *"drum sergeant."*

**lead stroke.** See *"drum sergeant."*

**leumluath.** Also called a "grip." Series of notes: melody note, Low-G, D grace note, Low-G, back to melody note. Prounced *"lem-loo-ah."*

**LG.** *(abbreviation)* Low G. Somewhat uncommon in usage.

**light D-throw.** See *"D-throw."*

**light music.** Any tune that is not a piobaireachd. Sometimes referred to as "ceol beag," meaning "little music" in Gaelic.

**Li'l Mac.** A brand of blowpipe flapper valve, a capped black plastic tapered cylinder that fits into the bore at the base of the blowpipe.

## M

**mace.** The shoulder-high decorative staff, ornamented with a metallic sphere at the top, carried by a drum major and used to signal the main body of his/her band.

**manometer.** An instrument used to measure pressure in the terms of "inches of water." A typical set of bagpipes will require between 20-40 inches of water to sound. A dial manometer looks like a gauge and simply fits into the top of one of the drones—or attached to a hose so one can pipe and view the gauge at the same time. A water manometer is a long tube partially filled with water of which one end is fitted to the top of one of the drones. *[Elsewhere on this site: How to Make a Bagpipe Water Manometer.]*

**march.** 1) *(noun)* A type of tune. 2) *(verb)* To walk in an organized fashion, typically with the rest of a band.

**march past.** See *"massed bands."*

**mark.** Another name for "version," used with a number after the "mark," usually in roman numerals, such as "Brand X chanter, mark III." These different versions are typically in a series over time and may or may not be noted as such by the manufacturer. Abbreviated "Mk."

**massed bands.** A combined performance of two or more (but usually all available) bands at some event. Also called a "march past" in Scotland.

**Maxville.** In Ontario, Canada, this is the location of the North American Championships.

**MBE.** *(abbreviation)* Member of the Order of the British Empire. A British distinguished honor. A lesser honor than OBE. *Also see "BEM" and "OBE."*

**medley.** A series of tightly unified tunes played as at one time.

**melody pipe.** A less common name for a chanter. See "*chanter.*"

**metric value.** Refers to the mathmatical time that a played note takes in terms of a musical score. For instance, gracenotes have no metric value, that is, they are not counted in a bar toward the total time for the bar—mathmatically, they are considered to take no time.
(Gracenotes have musical value though.)
Melody notes do have metric value.

**metronome.** An instrument for keeping time when practicing. Old mechanical style included a metal rod which would tip left and right from a pivot point at the bottom. More accurate modern digital metronomes include flashing indicators, a reference tone, volume controls and other features.

**military pleating.** See "*stripe.*"

**mini fly plaid.** A long piece of tartan material—approximately a foot wide by 4-1/2 feet long—that is draped over the left shoulder with a brooch at the front, attached at the waist in the rear and secured by buttoning a hidden loop to the epaulet button. Somewhat uncommon. *Also see "fly plaid."*

**Mk.** *(abbreviation)* Mark. See *"mark."*

**Montrose doublet.** One particular style of coublet, this is a close-fitting formal jacket with a large fabric panel covering the chest, held in place by vertical rows of buttons on the left and right. Napolean Bonapart is often depicted wearing one of these.

**mounts.** In the most basic sense, the items "mounted" to the wood on a set of pipes, that is, the trimmings. Includes the ferrules, the bushes, the projecting mounts. *Also see "projecting mounts."*

**mouth.** The opening located at the top of a chanter reed, formed by two opposing pieces of cane.

**mouth piece.** A tubular piece of wood or plastic that screws onto the threaded end of the blowpipe and fits into the piper's mouth.

**M.S.** *(abbreviation)* Manuscript. Typically referring hand-written sheet music.

**M.S.R.** *(abbreviation)* March, Strathesby, Reel. Common combination of tunes played in competition.

**M.S.S.** *(abbreviation)* Manuscripts. Typically referring hand-written sheet music.

# N

**National Piping Centre.** A year around bagpiping school based in Glasgow, Scotland.

**Northern Gathering.** A high profile competition held annually in Inverness, Scotland.

**NPC.** *(abbreviation)* National Piping Centre. *See "National Piping Centre."*

**NRV.** *(abbreviation)* Non-return valve. Used in the blowpipe to prevent air from escaping back out from the bag. *See "blowpipe valve."*

**NSP.** *(abbreviation)* Northumbrian Small Pipes.

# O

**Oban.** A town in Scotland, home of the Argyllshire Gathering. *Also see "Argyllshire Gathering."*

**OBE.** *(abbreviation)* Officer of the Order of the British Empire. A British distinguished honor. A greater honor than MBE. *Also see "BEM" and "MBE."*

**open note.** An undesirable note in which a finger is incorrectly raised on a hole below the top open hole. For instance, an "open C" would mean the piper has the low-A hole open instead of correctly closed with his/her pinky finger.

**open piper.** "Open" in this context refers to the grade status of the piper. "Open" is the top grade, also known as "professional." *Also see "grade."*

**overtone.** *See "harmonic."*

**P**

**parlor pipes.** Mouth-blown Highland smallpipes (a scaled-down highland bagpipe).

**PEI.** *(abbreviation)* Prince Edward Island. Location of the second College of Piping in Canada, which is affiliated with the original COP located in Glasgow, Scotland.

**pibroch.** A somewhat accepted misspelling of piobaireachd. See *"piobaireachd."*

**pick up note(s).** A note or short series of introductory notes preceeding a part of a tune, and usually do not compose a complete bar of music. Most commonly found at the beginning of a tune. These notes are not included in any repeat of the part.

**pìob mhór.** Means "a bagpipe" in Scottish. Pronouced *"peep vore."* You may also see **"a' phìob-mhór"** which means "the bagpipe" and is pronounced *"uh feep vore."*

**piobaire.** Means "bagpiper" in Scottish. Pronounced *"PEEP-uh-thuh."*

**piobaireachd.** *(noun)* Used to describe the traditional music of the pipes, sometimes referred to as "the classical music of the pipes." Composed of a ground (or "urlar") which is the first part of the tune, followed by doublings and or variations which substitute embellishments or phrases for those that appear in the ground, then the tune returns to end with the ground or a portion thereof. (Some piobaireachds call for the urlar to be played between each doubling/variation movement.) Complete piobaireachd tunes typically run 6 to 15 minutes in length. Sometimes referred to as "ceol mor." In Scottish, the term "piobaireachd" roughly means "bagpipe music" or "bagpiping." Pronounced *"pee-brock."*

**piobaireachd high-G.** A slightly flatter high-G note often times used then playing piobaireachd, which is sounded like a typical high-G but altered by holding the F hole closed with the top hand middle finger.

**PiobMaster.** A brand of bagpipe music notation software made by CeolMor Software. [website]

**pipe chanter.** See *"chanter."*

**pipe corporal.** See *"Lance Corporal."*

**pipe major.** Head piper and leader of a pipe band. Often seen abbreviated as "PM." Usually marches in the frontmost, rightmost position.

**pipe sergeant.** Pipe major's right-hand man. Normally assists in tuning, teaching, etc. Fills in when pipe major is absent. Often seen abbreviated as "PS", "P/S", or "P/Sgt".

**piper.** Shorter version of "bagpiper."

**piper's plaid.** A very long length of plaid material wrapped diagonally around the chest area and hung over the left shoulder down to about 6-8 inches off the ground. Used with formal dress. Also known as a "full plaid."

**pitch.** *(noun)* The sharpness or flatness of a sound, describing the frequency of the sound waves.

**plaid.** 1) Fabric woven of differently colored yarns in a perpendicular pattern. Prounced *"plad."* Not all plaids are tartans. 2) Long, rectangular piece of fabric usually worn over the left shoulder. Prounced *"played."*

**playing up.** In competition, if an individual or band competes in a grade level more advanced that the grade of which they are part, this is considered "playing up," i.e. A registered Grade IV player competes in a Grade III event at a games. Rules vary association to association, some prohibit playing up and restrict a player/band to a predetermined grade.

**PM, P/M, P.M.** *(abbreviation)* Pipe major. *See "pipe major."*

**pointed playing.** Where every 2 or 4 beats is held slightly longer than the notes inbetween, slightly altering the tune from what is written to increase contrast of notes. This term usually applies to jigs, reels and strathspeys, such as "pointed jig." *Also see "round playing."*

**Poly.** *(abbreviation)* Polypenco. *See "Polypenco."*

**Polypenco.** This synthetic (a polymer) is used as a replacement for traditional wood in the manufacture of bagpipes and practice chanters. Polypenco is a registered trademark of Quadrant Engineering Plastic Products, Inc. *Also see "Delrin."*

**popcorn top.** A pronounced "checker board" texture weave at the top of hose. Typically a separate piece of attire (a cuff) that is slipped over the top of the hose, but may also be integrated into the hose itself. *Also see "cuff."*

**POTD.** *(abbreviation)* Piper of the Day. An honor sometimes awarded to the most successful competition piper at a games, in a particular grade or otherwise.

**practice chanter.** A small simple mouth blown double-reed instrument (similar to a recorder) with the fingering of a full set of Great Highland Bagpipes. Used for practicing fingering and learning new tunes. Often seen abbreviated as "PC."

**practice pipes.** Mouth-blown bagpipe with small diameter brass tube drones and chanter.

**Prince Charlie jacket.** A formal jacket, commonly black or navy in color, high cut at the waist. Three large silver buttons adorn lower length of the sleeves and also left and right of the abdomen running appoximately vertically.

**professional piper.** 1) A bagpiper making his/her living from bagpiping. 2) A competing bagpiper in the highest competing grade, also called an "open piper." *Also see "grade."*

**projecting mounts.** The trim on the drones that sticks out—typically of wood, silver, ivory, or imitation ivory.

**PS, P/S, P.S., P/Sgt** *(abbreviation)* Pipe sergeant. *See "pipe sergeant."*

**PS.** *(abbreviation)* Piobaireachd Society. And in context could refer to the piobaireachd sheet music books compiled and published by the Piobaireachd Society, i.e. "That tune is in PS."

**pull-through.** A piece of fabric attached to a cord. Used for oiling drone bores.

# Q

**QMM.** *(abbreviation)* Quick March Medley. A series of march tunes used in competition.

**quartermaster.** Band Title. Individual responsible for the safety and accounting of a band's equipment. Arranges orders of new supplies as necessary. Can make available to the members a list of the minimum items and potential sources for those items needed to be in uniform. Attends all band officer meetings. Reports to the other officers.

# R

**reamer.** A tapered hand tool, appears much like a spike, used to broaden the bore of reed seats to allow a reed to sink deeper into the bore.

**red book.** Part 2 of The Highland Bagpipe Tutor by Seumas MacNeill and Thomas Pearston published by the College of Piping, Glasgow, Scotland. Discusses instrument maintenance, including reed selection and bag tie-in. Traditionally has been printed with a red cover. Part 1 has a green cover, Part 3 has a blue cover.

**reed.** *(noun)* A object with a vibrating surface that produces sound. One type is located in each of the drones, and another type is located in the chanter.

**reed cap.** A cover placed over a seated chanter reed to protect it while the chanter is removed from its stock. Sometimes called a "dry stock," "reed protector," or a "chanter cap."

**reed protector.** *See "reed cap."*

**reed seat.** The tapered hole located at the very top of the chanter or at the base of the drones into which fits a reed.

**reel.** *(noun)* A type of quick tune, usually in 2/2 time.

**regimental.** The condition of not wearing anything immediately under one's kilt. e.g. "It's going to be scorching tomorrow, I'm going regimental."

**REME.** *(abbreviation)* Royal Electrical and Mechanical Engineers. Part of the British Army. Pronounce "ree-mee."

**repousse.** A techinque of hammering designs into metal as an alternative to traditional engraving (removing/carving out material) typically seen in silver ferrules and slides.

**retreat.** A type of 3/4 march tune, historically played when one wanted your battling troops to turn around and escape the enemy.

**riffler file.** A metal "rat-tail file" tool with curved ends which is used to carve out chanter holes. Sometimes leaves a rough edge which can be finished off with a deburring tool. *Also see "deburring tool."*

**ring cap.** A circular piece of material inset into the bush at the top of a drone.

**RMMB.** *(abbreviation)* rec.music.makers.bagpipe. An Internet newsgroup, where users post messages, available through an Internet service provider's "news" server or though the web on Google.com's RMMB page.

**rodin.** A grip-like embellishment using B when coming from a C or D to a Low A: melody note followed by Low-G, B, Low-G, Low-A. Pronounced *"ROE-din."*

**roll-off.** A series of drum rolls that precedes the strike-in by a band. *Also see "strike in."*

**round playing.** Where the notes on the beat are not held out longer than the notes inbetween the beats in any noticeable fashion, that is, the notes are "even" or equal value. This term usually applies to jigs, reels and strathspeys, such as "round jig." Playing a tune "round" can also mean evening out different valued notes so that they are more equal, for instance, reducing contrast been a dotted eighth and an adjacent sixteenth note. *Also see "pointed playing."*

**row.** Refers to a band in formation, the line of players arranged side by side. (As opposed to a file.)

**RSM.** *(abbreviation)* Regimental Sergeant Major.

**rush.** A wire or similar object inserted into an acoustic chamber (such as the interior of a drone reed) to alter the associated pitch. Sometimes, but very rarely, used in piping.

**RVM.** *(abbreviation)* The Silver Medal of The Royal Victorian Order. An award presented by the royal family of England.

## S

**sash.** *See "duty sash."*

**SCA.** *(abbreviation)* Society for Creative Anacronism. Not a piping organization, but this group of people dressing up and reenacting various time periods (usually middle-ages to 1700s) will sometimes include pipers and as such, come up in conversion.

**Schreger pattern.** A series of crossing lines found in real ivory which can be used to identify which animal the ivory came from. Different animals have different crossing angles. Sometimes called "Schreger lines."

**Scottish Piping Society of London, The.** Based in London, this charity organization was founded in 1932 to promote the GHB in the region. Sponsors the annual *Bratach Gorm* competition.

**season.** *(verb)* To add a substance to the bag to control moisture and act as a fungicide.

**seasoning.** *(noun)* Substance added to a hide bag to help make it airtight, control moisture, and act as a fungicide. Honey was once commonly used as a seasoning.

**seat.** *See "[reed seat](#)."*

**seconds.** A second arrangement of a tune played by a piper (or some small number) in a multiple piper setting that typically includes harmonies or otherwise enhances the main body of the tune. A complex band tune can also include thirds, fourths, etc.

**set.** A few tunes that are consistently played together as a group. These groupings can be decided by any individual and are not predetermined by an association or other entity, though some competitions require a series of specific types of tunes, such as an [MSR](#).

**sett.** One "unit" of the repeating tartan pattern. "To the sett," one of two ways how a kilt can be pleated, means the kilt shows the entire tartan pattern when in resting position (overlapping pleats). As opposed to "to the stripe." *Also see "<u>stripe</u>."*

**setting.** A version of a tune.

**SFU.** *(abbreviation)* <u>Simon Fraser University Pipe Band</u>. A Grade I band based in British Columbia, Canada.

**SG.** *(abbreviation)* Scots Guards. Usually refers to one of the SG volumes of pipe tune settings, can be seen in context of "SG 1" or SG 2 " for example. The Scots Guards is a UK military regiment that in 1953 standardized hundreds of piping tunes by publishing their "Standard Settings of Pipe Music."

**sgian dubh.** A small knife worn in the sock of a piper. Literally translated it means "black knife," though many believe "black" referred to "hidden" or "bad" instead of its shade. Sometimes seen spelled "sgean dubh" or "sqian dubh" or "skean dubh." Pronounced *"skeen doo."*

**shake.** A less common term with the same meaning as "tap" or "strike." *Also see "<u>strike</u>."*

**sharp.** A note is considered *sharp* if it is above (higher sounding than) the expected pitch.

**sheep skin.** One of several materials commonly used for bagpipe bags. Requires frequent seasoning, usually lasts 18-24 months, allows moisture to escape quickly from the bag.

**Sherifmuire.** A type of doublet. Not as common.

**shoulder.** The area across the central potion of the exposed cane on a chanter reed. On a ridge cut reed, the shoulder is quite pronounced.

**shuttle pipes.** Bagpipes characterized by drones being integrated into a single cylinder about a foot long with sliding tabs for tuning.

**side drum.** See *"snare drum."*

**signature.** See *"time signature."*

**siubhal.** The name applied to a piobaireachd variation if it meets the following criteria: long low-A, B or low-G note is followed by a short theme note. The long note is preceded by a G gracenote. The short theme note is preceded by an E gracenote, except E and F (G gracenote), high-G (thumb gracenote), and high-A (no gracing). A siubhal variation is played in a round manner. In Gaelic, "siubhal" means a moving, traveling and can also mean dying. Pronouced "SHOO-ul." Also see "siubhal doubling."

**siubhal doubling.** The name applied to a piobaireachd variation if it meets the same criteria as a siubhal, *but* instead of a long low-A being played, a short note same as the following theme note is played. "Siubhal" is pronouced "SHOO-ul." See "siubhal."

**skilt.** A coined term for a kilted skirt, a women's clothing item.

**skirl.** 1) *(verb)* To play the bagpipe. [general public]; 2) *(verb)* squealing, as in "it's unstable, it tends to skirl on low-A" [piper-specific]; 3) *(noun)* The sound of a bagpipe, a shrill cry [public].

**slainte.** A toast of sorts, in Gaelic meaning "health," "to your health," "to good health." Used much like a Brit might use "cheers."

**slide.** See "tuning slide."

**slip jig.** A quick type of tune with the time signature of 9/8.

**slow air.** A slow type of tune, sometimes used in a sense synonymous with "slow march," other times it's used to describe a tune with which you can take liberties with the tempo, such as holding notes beyond what would be appropriate to maintain the beat. *Also see "slow march."*

**slow march.** A slow type of tune, sometimes used in a sense synonymous with "slow air," but it is generally accepted that you have to maintain the beat and not take liberties with the tempo. *Also see "slow air."*

**slur.** Sliding a finger off of (or onto) a hole to gradually raise (or lower) the pitch to another note.

**small pipes.** A bellows-blown set of pipes with very thin diameter drones and chanter. The drones share a common stock and can sometimes include a baritone drone as well as a tenor and bass. Typically played from a sitting position.

**snare drum.** High pitched drum that maintains the beat, played in a horizontal position with two hard drum sticks. Gets its name from the rattling snares strung across the bottom head. Also called a "side drum."

**sock top.** See *"cuff."*

**sole.** A disk-like adornment at the bottom of a chanter, usually composed of ivory, imitation ivory, or silver.

**sound box.** The space inside of a reed that is located between the top of the binding and the shoulder.

**spats.** Worn over the shoes and extend above the ankle, typically white in color with buttons up the side. Usually only worn with elaborate highland attire.

**SPBA.** *(abbreviation)* Saskatchewan Pipe Band Association. www.gpfn.sk.ca/culture/arts/spba/index.html. Scottish Pipe Band Association, now called the Royal Scottish Pipe Band Association (RSPBA).

**SPSL.** *(abbreviation)* The Scottish Piping Society of London.

**sporran.** A purse-like object worn in front of a kilt. Dress sporrans, such as a horse hair sporran, do not always have storage space.

**springing.** As in "springing a tongue." On a cane drone reed, sometimes if the reed does not sound easily, if the tongue is sprung (or pulled up and released) it may remedy the problem. Is often not recommended on a synthetic drone reed, but depends on the tongue material.

**SPSL.** *(abbreviation)* Scottish Piping Society of London.

**SR.** *(abbreviation)* Strathesby, Reel. Combination of tunes played in competition, though not as common as the MSR. *Also see "MSR."*

**SSP.** *(abbreviation)* Scottish Small Pipes. *Also see "small pipes."*

**stand.** More or less, another name for "set," used in context, "a stand of pipes."

**staple.** The cylindrical/conical piece of metal at the base of a chanter reed, typically copper or brass that provides a support for the blades.

**static grace note.** A grace note in a movement that is sounded when lowering a finger other than the finger associated with that note, for example, the "E" grace note in an E doubling. As opposed to a "active grace note." This somewhat uncommon term is seen in *The College of Piping Tutor For The Highland Bagpipe: Part 3*. Also see "*active grace note.*"

**STB.** *(abbreviation)* Scotland the Brave. Extremely common piping tune.

**steward.** An individual responsible for coordinating a single competition event, typically one is assigned to a particular "boards" or judging area.

**sticks.** Refers to a set of drones, stocks and a blowpipe. New sets of bagpipes can often be purchased as just "sticks" to which you would add your own bag, chanter and reeds.

**stock.** A collar (typically wood, but sometimes plastic) that is attached to ("tied into") the bag into which fits either the blowpipe, chanter or drones.

**strathspey.** A type of dance tune, has a very heavy "swing." Usually in a 4/4 time signature. Pronouced *"straths pay."*

**street band.** A band that doesn't compete, may or may not be involved with its regional association.

**strike.** A quick "slap" (sounding a grace note) with one or more fingers to a lower note then back up. Also called a "tap" or "hit" and more rarely a "shake" or "echo."

**strike-in.** The action of striking the bag in conjunction with blowing to start the drones.

**stripe.** One of two ways how a kilt can be pleated. To the stripe means the kilt shows the main stripe of the tartan at the edge of each pleat when in resting position (overlapping pleats) instead of showing the complete tartan pattern. Sometimes referred to as "military pleating" and is a little more common with bands. Depending on the tartan, some kilts pleated to the stripe may show an entirely different color when pleats are swinging open. Also called pleating "to the line." As opposed to "to the sett." *Also see "sett."*

**suite.** A single tune composed of parts of different style elements, for example a tune that starts with a slow air and moves into hornpipe passage then into a strathspey. Not to be confused with a medley or set composed of different tunes.

# T

**T.** *(abbreviation)* Taorluath. Used in the context of music notation for piobaireachd. Rather than writing out the notes for all the taorluath embellishments in a taorluath variation, a letter "T" is used.

**tachum.** A short B or C note followed by a D gracenote down to a lower note. Pronounced *"tay-kum."*

**tam.** A broad brimless, and somewhat formless, hat of Irish/Scottish origins. Drapes off to one side or to the back, much like an oversized French beret. In 1791, Robert Burns wrote a poem titled "Tom O'Shanter" from which this gets its name. Also called a "tammy" or a "tam o'shanter."

**tam o'shanter.** *See "tam."*

**tammy.** *See "tam."*

**taorluath.** A combination of grace notes forming an embelishment. For example: melody note, followed by Low-G, D, Low-G, E, then ending on a melody note. In Gaelic, "luath" means "quick." Prounced *"tar-loo-ah."*

**taorluath a mach.** Only executed from B, C and D. *(Full details would be long and convoluted, consult your instructor or book.)* Prounced *"tar-loo-ah ah-mahk"*

**taorluath doubling.** A doubling variation that is played with taorluaths. Term applies to piobaireachd tunes.

**tap.** *See "strike."*

**tartan.** A specific pattern of plaid associated with a particular clan. Clans can have multiple tartans such as "ancient," "modern," or "hunting." *Also see "plaid."*

**tassel.** Found on each of the two ends of drone cords, these fabric bell-shaped ornaments with hanging fringe keep the cords from coming undone. *Also see "drone cords."*

**tenon.** Each section of a bagpipe fitting that is covered with hemp: the tuning slides, the base of the drone/blowpipe that fits into the stock, the top of the chanter. This comes from a general woodworking term describing a cut into the end of a piece of wood.

**tenor drone.** One the two short drones on a set of bagpipes, when tuned sounds exactly one octave lower than Low-A on the chanter.

**tenor drum.** Medium pitched drum, played while held in a horizontal position with two fuzzy mallets that are typically twirled with flair by the drummer.

**themal.** Refers to a note that is not gracing another note, an "important" note in the tune that would significantly alter the tune if removed.

**thick.** As in a "thick note." A note that is slightly and intentionally flat, such as might be used on high-A. Used in context: "I like my high-A a little thick."

**third hand.** A tuning aid for beginning pipers, this device fits onto the chanter to cover the B-C-D holes allowing the lower hand to be free to tune the drones to low-A.

**throat.** See *"sound box."*

**throw on D.** See *"D-throw."*

**tie-in.** *(verb)* To cut holes and attach stocks to a bagpipe bag using some type of cord material. As in "Tie-in a bag."

**time.** See *"time signature."*

**time signature.** Every written tune indicates the time signature at the beginning of the tune by a fraction. The top figure indicates the number of beats in a bar. The bottom figure indicates the length of the note that constitutes each beat, which is expressed in fractions of a whole note. For example, 2/4 indicates two beats in each bar with a quarter note equaling one beat; 6/8 indicates six beats in each bar which an eighth note equaling one beat.

**tone.** A state of a set of pipes being in perfect harmony. Such as "playing tone."

**tone box.** *See "sound box."*

**tongue.** The vibrating surface of a reed.

**trailing drones.** The undesireable situation when the drones gradually drop in pitch at the end of a tune rather than simply going silent. *Also see "cut off."*

**trap.** *See "water trap."*

**trews.** A style of full-length tartan trousers.

**triplet.** Three notes that are given the value of one beat. Indicated on sheet music by an arch linking the first and third notes with a small "3" indicated underneath.

**tune.** 1) *(noun)* A piece of music. Music for the bagpipes are not typically referred to as "songs." 2) *(verb)* To adjust a drone or the position of a hole in a chanter to achieve the desired pitch.

**tuner.** A device that registers a sound's pitch (or frequency), usually in Hertz (Hz). Used to tune the drones to the chanter or set the chanter pitch.

**tuning phrase.** A series of notes used to determine if the bagpipes in tune. For a solo piper, this could be a short but complex series of random-sounding notes. For a band, it could be a simple note or two followed by the full scale.

**tuning pin.** A thinner diameter portion of the drone over which an upper portion of the drone fits and adjusts for tuning. Also called a "slider."

**tuning screw.** A threaded insert at the unseated end of a synthetic drone reed that alters the pitch of the reed when screwed in or out. Invented by Mark Wygent to replace the tuning/end plug. *Also see "end plug."*

**tuning slide.** An ornamental metal—typically silver or nickel or brass—cylindical fitting around a tuning pin. *See "tuning pin."*

**turner.** An individual who carves out bagpipe parts on a lathe. *Also see "lathe."*

**turning.** The action of carving a bagpipe part while it is rotating on a lathe. *Also see "lathe."*

**U**

**uilleann pipes.** Irish bellows driven bagpipes. Pronouced *"ILL-un."*

**urlar.** See *"ground."*

# V

**valve.** See *"blowpipe valve"* or *"drone valve."*

**variation.** A part in a piobaireachd tune where some notes or embellishments are substituted for others that appear in the ground. A piobaireachd many have several variations and/or doublings. *Also see "piobaireachd."*

**vent.** Hole located on the left and right sides of the chanter below the Low-G hole.

**vocable.** A human speakable word-like group of sounds associated with a note or group of notes. Can be either a formal system or spontaneous usuage. For instance, when singing along with a tune "dum dee dum bum" would be considered vocables, as the canntaireachd is also considered. *Also see "canntaireachd."*

# W

**war pipes.** Usually short for Irish War Pipes. See *"Irish war pipes."*

**water manometer.** *See "manometer."*

**water trap.** Either a rudimentary device (such as a cork with a metal tube passed through it) placed in the base of the blowpipe stock or a more elaborate tubing system with a canister filled with dessicant. Used by wet blowers or in humid environments.

**wet blower.** A piper who introduces a lot of moisture to the bag when playing, sometimes requiring a water trap or bag that permits moisture to evaporate easily, such as a sheepskin bag. *Also see "water trap."*

**wheel.** A turn executed by a band in which the players on the inside of the turn march with a smaller stride and the outer players march with a longer stride in order to maintain a straight row.

www.ingramcontent.com/pod-product-compliance
Lightning Source LLC
Chambersburg PA
CBHW071412040426
**42444CB00009B/2218**